Praise for *The Aest*

Roger Armbrust's contemporary sonnets plunge right to the core of both the matter and the reader. Through sound, vision and a plain-spoken voice, these accessible sonnets create an immediate resonance within, bringing this poetic form to the everyday reader and begging each one to be read over and over again.

RAYMOND HAMMOND, EDITOR, *The New York Quarterly*

Roger Armbrust packs a tremendous amount of movement into fourteen lines. This bobbing, weaving, trembling, shaking collection is long overdue!

AMY FUSSELMAN, AUTHOR OF *8* AND *The Pharmacist's Mate*

I have known and admired Roger Armbrust's poems for many years. But when Roger met the sonnet . . . he quickly turned the window-like form into a window on a world—his. And what a rich, varied world it is. In the sonnet "Spring 2007 Evocations" he writes about his daughter's art. With a few substitutions in pronouns it might read: ". . . I marvel how he's trusted/his heart, his growing skills of artistic eye/and graceful hand, transforming emotions/and intelligence into sonnets." This is not to suggest all of the poems are delicate—they often display muscular rhythms and playful rimes—but he knows when they need to be just that.

H. A. MAXSON, POET, AUTHOR OF *On the Sonnets of Robert Frost: A Critical Examination of the 37 Poems*

THE AESTHETIC ASTRONAUT

ALSO BY ROGER ARMBRUST

How To Survive (poems)

Final Grace (chapbook)

THE
AESTHETIC
ASTRONAUT

Sonnets by

Roger Armbrust

Parkhurst Brothers
Little Rock

Printed in the United States of America

Design by Randall Williams

This book is printed on archival-quality paper which meets the standards
for durability and longevity as established by ANSI.

12 11 10 9 8 7 6 5 4 3 2 1

The Library of Congress PCCN: 2008909924
ISBN 13: 978-1-935166-00-9
ISBN 10: 1-935166-00-x

Parkhurst Brothers, Inc., Publishers
415 North McKinley Street, Suite 280-J
Little Rock, Arkansas 72205
www.pbros.net

PBIpn002. dop032009

To my brother Frank,

his wife Kay,

and my sister Joan,

with love and thanks

for their love through the years.

CONTENTS

Writing Sonnets

A simple process really. Rilke said
if you must write, use your experience,
imagination, and dreams. Rob Frost made
it American, blending sound and sense
of everyday speech. Shakespeare, critics say,
did it best. His sonnets flower with grace
of image, heart, wisdom, rhyme and wordplay,
caressing the ear's most sensitive place
like a whispering lover. I try to
recall those teachers each time I click on
the computer, feel the Muse's breath flow
like warm mist around me. "Well?" she questions,
softly tapping her foot, inviting verse.
So, I write. Hardly perfect. Could be worse.

BLUE LIGHT

for Chris Allen

Winter evenings just after sunset,
my future father would stride athletic
under and beyond that lone blue light set
back from locked doors, dark windows, pathetic
white walls of the asylum, and through chilled
Little Rock night, a cocky bachelor
orderly, making his way to her, filled
with a young man's hope for touch, for smiles, for
heaven's laughter glowing in her hazel
eyes. My future mother, ears a bee's hum
from a day's work on the switchboard at Bell,
would blot her lipstick with Kleenex, succumb
to admiring mirrors, ponder and sigh,
awaiting fiery blue light of his eyes.

COME YE BACK

Internet radio flows Loreena
McKennitt's soprano semi-whisper,
transforming to Celtic St. John of the
Cross's images of dark night's specter,
haunting strings framing her mystical voice.
Beyond those strings, my mother is singing
her soft, a cappella, eternal choice
of Irish legend she loved while living:
gentle plea to young Danny to return
when summer's in the meadow. She would hold
my child's frame close, quiet my crying yearn
to end the toothache, or my coughing cold,
rocking me to cloudlike silence with her
own, then-young, soprano semi-whisper.

My daughter, diving deep into her art,
forms abstract patterns—hand-dyed and rusted
silk, mixed media, weaved stitching all part
of each work. I marvel how she's trusted
her heart, her growing skills of artist's eye
and graceful hands, transforming emotion
and intelligence onto fiber. I
see this as poet, steeped in devotion
to art as blessed images, spirit's prize.
I see this as father, recalling how,
at age four, she caught us by such surprise
with her finger painting, (I'm smiling now)
her mom and I soared in its dimension.
We framed and hung it in our Polk Street den.

EDITING SHAKESPEARE

A birthday sonnet for Catherine, my daughter

In her rendition of Prospero's Speech,
Loreena McKennitt edits Shakespeare.
The Bard's protagonist, his magic reach
ended, judges himself a prisoner
of the audience, calls his soul "confined."
The singer alters the word to "released,"
casting her listener, perhaps, a kind
jailer compared to ancestors who'd feast
on Will's charmed words in Elizabethan
days. A worthy action for an artist
wishing to end her CD with élan
vital, much as the Creator once kissed
Adam with breath. Much as a father holds
his daughter close, protecting her from cold.

August 21, 2007

Night of the Hunter

William Packard, my creative mentor,
often lamented to his poetry
classes how Manhattan's night sky tortured
artists: grazing herds of stars fallen prey
to those two voracious wolves—smog and lights.
Through years of walking Greenwich Village streets
or Washington Square Park, we'd cherish nights
when Venus peeked through. Seldom we'd just greet
the moon. Once, through winter's bitter cold, I
limped lonely past NYU's library,
turned on LaGuardia, looked up and sighed,
"Oh, my. Hello." Orion's glow carried
clear and bright as lovers' eyes down to mine.
I felt caressed, warmed, lost in the divine.

September 11, 2001

for William Packard

The day before your sixth birthday, Auden
wrote of sitting in a dive observing
a city caught up in fear and awe. When
he did, I suppose someone was serving
you dinner miles away, Mamaroneck,
pre-party promises as you slurped ade
while Auden sipped ale, alone in the dark
bar's corner, napkin stained with words he made
stand at attention in eleven-line
stanzas. Some thirty years later, he told
you he had disowned those verses: a fine
line he had drawn for truth. Now, on this cold,
evil day, after you've turned sixty-eight,
we smell death, feel pain, can call his lines great.

Three-Man Weave

On basketball courts at Catholic High
and LRU, our practiced discipline
found graceful motion: two teammates and I
stretched the hardwood's width, so at ease within
our moves, timed with leather sphere passed from man
to man. We'd catch and toss with fingertips
(never the palms), flicking our flash-quick hands
as if swatting gnats, our shoes' rubber grips
yelping as they bit and released waxed floor,
passer cutting behind receiver, each
body barely missing each. I adored
the drill's court-length curves, my ultimate reach
to the goal. We swayed as an entity.
Our dance, I see now, formed infinity.

IVALEA

The first time I saw her, she stood graceful
as a Victorian porcelain, shy
and still at the high-school party, tasteful
blue dress accenting her eyes of clear sky.
We danced. Amazed by her beauty, I sensed
irony of fragile strength in her touch,
intense intelligence in her silence.
Through those awkward months, I liked her so much,
my heartbeat dulled my head. I'd turned and she'd
vanished. Forty years have flown, yet I've saved
her soft smile. Last year, I learned she had died.
I'd like to go to Mayfield, find her grave,
listen and talk to her. Breathe in tranquil,
clear air. I'm praying that someday I will.

IVALEA II

I couldn't take her to my senior prom.
Catholic High rules: Only St. Mary's
girls. She went to Hall. I opted to come
to the post-dance bash; shucked the main soiree.
Weeks later, patient as ocean, she sat
through my graduation; later caressed
my hand with the gift: a medal of Saint
Christopher, her name and the date impressed
on its back. I cherish it still. These years
later, I've blocked how it ended, or why.
But my mind often sees her smiling, hears
her soft voice. Betsy said, before she died,
she left this brief note: *Please don't forget me.*
It's clear to me now my heart won't let me.

The Engineer's Proposal

And so this bridge we call relationship,
we agree, must rest on concrete columns
of honesty driven deep by our lips
forming words humble as earth. Support comes
through trusses of caress, both vertical
and diagonal angling of arms and
firm legs, latched to ironic chords—gentle
hands with strong grasp, air-light feet to command
the dance. We'll weld these to beams of hope, keep
joints secured with caring acts (holding doors,
sharing chores). Cement our surface with deep
layers of faith, center striped in contours
of reflection and prayer, seeking the key
to insure our grounding in honesty.

"A Spiritual Canticle of the Soul and the Bridegroom Christ"

for Jessica and Wilfrid

In the sixteenth century, St. John of
the Cross, imprisoned at Toledo in
a windowless cell, sensed light from above
beaming through a loophole. So he'd begin
his office, honoring that hour of sight
until the sun's eye had closed, leaving him
in the tight-walled dark, listening to fights
below: muffled voices swirling their rims
of anger in defiance and defense
of St. Teresa. Somehow those rhythms
lifted him to poetry: a conscience
consenting to union with God—soft hymns
with images of bride and groom, like you,
uniting in sacred love only two

souls can find through surrendering themselves.
A love released only when humans choose
to open wide their own dark, tight-walled cells
and let in light of another life whose
light only came with the opening: sense
and spirit moving toward what St. John called
"overflowing mystical intelligence."
Now sense and spirit blend here, at St. Paul's,
where we pause to honor that hour of Sight
recognizing your vow's continuum
beyond space and time, beyond peace and plight
lovers with faith seem to accept with some
strength beyond courage. Your marriage frames it.
But even St. John couldn't explain it.

October 13, 2001

Light My Fire

I still recall smooth sweep of her brown hair—
guarded from her sad eyes by a small clip—
blended with strands hinting of golden flare,
ends too short to touch her shoulders. Her lips
lost to any smile. Having just broken
up with some guy, fueling her self-pity
with Jack Daniels, she had barely spoken.
Our first date, I juggled and tossed witty
words to her. Ignored, they fell and shattered
at her feet. Feliciano began
his haunting "Light My Fire." Like a tattered
coat, she crumpled in a corner chair, ran
her finger along the glass rim. She hummed
Jose's song as his ghostly guitar strummed.

Years before in high school, I had admired
her from afar, like da Vinci's lady.
But, oh, this college-party night, afire
with longing, I hoped to hold her, maybe
kiss like surprised lovers. But no. I whipped
down brews in revenge, ignored my despair
at her rejection. Laughed. Danced. Then I tripped
away, drunken Caliban; left her there
alone. The staggered streets of Fayetteville
sprinkled couples from frat houses and dorms
where '60s music blared caustic and shrill.
Their laughter beat down my slurred threats of harm.
Missing her, I cursed the night: frigid, starry.
Years later, I wish I could say I'm sorry.

Ice Cube

Light flows so intensely through this frozen
crystal prism, faintest color's our result:
gray haze like London morning's explosion
of mist and smoke; then suddenly occult
transforming to translucence at center,
as clear as psyche following prayer.
Adjusting to this sculpture of winter,
the eye finds at its core a small layer
of droplets suspended like rain, or tears,
timeless reminder of what cleanses earth
and us. It chills the palm, predicts our years
to come: our living, dying, and rebirth.
Months from now, we'll consider how we felt,
passing it hand to hand, watching it melt.

When Love Was a Fudgesicle

When love was a fudgesicle shaped like a
frosted, mud-coated cathedral window
hoisted on a tongue depressor (say ahh),
we would nibble, lick, suck, and wonder how
its slick, dwindling mass still managed to melt,
stream with reckless speed down our tiny, pale
pirate's plank, drool and dry until it felt
like tar stuck on our thumbs and fingernails.
Palates and lips numb from cold, we'd bear all
suffering; result to scraping wet wood
with our teeth when those last stubborn lumps called
for risky measures. Sometimes splinters would
curl up, find a gum, take pain to new heights—
pinpoint omens of future lonely nights.

LIFE AS A DREAMSICLE

Our young senses swooned at surreal melding
of bright orange sherbet and vanilla
ice cream with a stick handle, slow melting
compared to sisters Fudge and Pop. Still, a
shudder of fear and wonder rose from us
when Creamsicle imposed its brief presence.
Our palates found no match for Dream's promise,
Cream's ice-milk dermis (watery essence)
a poor player next to our favorite's
velvety inner flesh. And now, high tech's
invaded our age—software composites
with Dreamsicle's moniker, meant to work
in Walkman phones, threatening our dreamy shtick,
forcing humans to listen before we lick.

SHE

Perhaps because it's August she rises
in my mind and heart like sudden summer
rain. Memory's swift torrent surprises
me, shaking the past from peaceful slumber.
Shower of images and echoes. Yes,
August, when we first began to sense our
special love, growing as a soft caress
flowers into naked passion, power
vested in vulnerable trust. Our eyes
opened slow as newborn kittens', happy
to discover the world. Yet fear's disguise
can fool lovers, its veiled claws carve deeply
in each psyche. It had before we met.
Our sad parting still fills me with regret.

The Trouble with Clear Weather

Here's the problem: each day of cloudless sky
when I gaze up at limitless azure,
I remain caught by pure glow of your eyes
that night I first kissed your perfect lips, sure
you'd step away, a queen enflamed by her
insensitive gift. You stayed. Studied me
like a scientist both puzzled and stirred
by her new discovery. "Oh, so we
are doing this," you whispered, as if caught
up in some chemistry experiment.
Research approved, you turned, began to trot
downstairs, looked back to smile with contentment,
then dashed to catch the D Train to Brooklyn.
On the Village bus, I just sat and grinned.

Spirits Burning Bright

On your CD, you sing of bright burning
spirits watching over love, ghosts come to
claim you. I still recall the day, learning
of their presence as you spoke of some who
watched us touch, kiss, hold, move through love rhythms
as we watched each other's spirit open
day by night. I can't blame you for schisms
in our psyches, for your losing hope in
our love, or how you had to swim away,
dive deep into breathless dark, having to
find phantoms before singing of their sway
over us. I only know loving you
couldn't save you from the dark. How I'd pray
you'd find light; how I pray it to this day.

PORTRAIT

The Nikon film camera dresses your
head like an ebony and silver crown,
your composed hands aiming its aperture
at the bathroom mirror. Dark hair flows down
past your shoulders, rests in swirls on wide crests
of your breasts, nipples teasing beige slip's lace.
Your slight stomach roll offers flesh caressed
by satin. I smile at how your calm gaze
recalls Napoleon when he declared
himself emperor, Pope Pius VII
slouched and frowning on his powerless chair,
eleven years before St. Helena,
isle named for the mother of Constantine.
Your sensual lips reflect Josephine's.

THE DANCE

Watching her video on YouTube, I
see her body sway and bounce at the mike,
easy moves to her bassist's rhythm—shy
yet sure singer's rocking the ride. It strikes
my heart. I recall years ago when we
dove into love—that swirling pool of fear,
laughter, long talks, intimate touches—free
to take chances, yet cautious as lost deer
in a dark wood. Her radio echoed
an old standard, Sinatra maybe. Bright
as a deejay, I chirped, "Hey, let's dance!" Slow
as syrup, she murmured, "I don't dance." Fright
froze her. I held her close. We barely moved.
Since then, she's gone a long way. I have, too.

Alone Together

This touch of hand on hand, this feeling of
flesh so much softer than satin, a warm
enclosure unequaled on earth. This love
expressed so simply, even witches' charms
can't match the hypnotic charge deep within
each cell's secret chamber, a space untapped
yet by science's mightiest probe, a den
of light, dark, calm, and storm fluid as sap,
flowing like lava, glowing like ancient
stars. How do we keep from tearing ourselves
into body parts? We lie still, patient
as roots of old trees, smiling like small elves
who share knowledge of treasure buried here,
close as our breathing, so distant from fear.

Mining

Swaziland's Lion Cave gave hematite
while Neanderthals carved flint for weapons
in Hungary. Green swirls of malachite
enthralled ancient Egyptians. Here, upon
Lake Superior's prehistoric shores,
underground chambers yielded copper, base
for tools and arrowheads. Now I explore
your body's rare ore as fingertips trace
rich veins of your limbs. Lips and tongue measure
your seams, moist walls of your mouth, its warm breath
inviting exploitation of treasure
in your loin's shaft, tender edge and depth
bare beneath our bed sheets. How we exclaim
in delight, feeling our dear earth reclaimed.

My Long Love Affair with Ketchup

Our intimate relationship with french
fries has proven a flexible ménage
à trois, linking us with that common wench
called hamburger, flaunting parsley corsage
of steak, even romping with turkey club
sandwiches. Remember times we've ambled
through power-breakfast platters? How we've rubbed
good eggs' elbows (preferably scrambled)?
At times I've suffered your independence,
like the night those mashed potatoes matched you
with green peas. You lacked any resistance,
or so it seemed, wanting me to catch you
mingling with those pods. I was at a loss,
spending the night with your cousin, shrimp sauce.

CHEDDAR CHEESE

In 1170, King Henry
pronounced your Somerset curdle yummy,
sharply praising your town's gifted gentry
who mixed raw milk, rennet from calves' tummies,
wrapping the coagulate in cloth, then
aging loaves in caves, like mankind itself.
But we've seen British tradition grow thin
in the States. Cheddar makers seeking pelf
now rely on genetics and fungus
Aspergillus niger, saving young cows.
Animal lovers dub that humongous
humaneness, or less bloody anyhow.
Vegetarian cheese chompers prefer
fig-tree bark or an evergreen creeper.

Last Night

And now honeysuckle's aroma; thick
as syrup, fills my nostrils like the breath
of my old lover on that night her slick
frame poured over me, just before her death,
her bourbon-coated whisper pleading first
for pain, then caress, then pain again, as
if she hoped for all before the end. Nursed
too long by my soft words, she cursed our last
lovemaking, the honeysuckle bouquet
I had brought to make peace. Neither of us
knew. Drunk, angry, again I lost my way:
A right sent her off the bed; her head just
missed the wrought-iron chair. She dressed, slammed the door.
The cop's call left me crying on the floor.

Omen

But those morning walks along the seashore—
grass like matted hair of some giant old
witch seeming to weave its way from her door
across landscape into salt water—told
her he'd return. Neither sun glinting like
gold-plated armor off the ocean's surge
nor bulky-cupped nests of loggerhead shrikes
would signal hope as she passed. Limestone urged
her on—a mammoth boulder to withstand
stormy tide, its sculpted titan's head ten
stories high, with scarred, gnarled, muscle-tense hand
of charcoal gray binding the left eye. Then
only the right's deep, dark socket aware,
she believed, of when he would join her there.

THE CREEK

The small creek slicing through Crestwood Manor
slides some thirty yards beside an asphalt
drive before diving like glazed eels under
brush and the road's curve, then rises to vault
crowds of rocks and weeds, primed to disappear
through dense trees of Allsopp Park. Even now,
after standing watch over brooks for years,
I marvel at each sparkling leap, laud how
pools between them stand still and smooth, tintype
frozen in time. With a hundred dwellings
framing the stream, litter's a minor gripe.
The maintenance crew keeps it from swelling.
A burly groundhog drinks there, bulk slouching
in slow retreat each time I'm approaching.

Nanoman

Watch the screen. Semi-clear cytoplasm
surrounds your cell's nucleus like River
Ocean. See within? Bridging its chasm
like thread-thin scaffolds? That flexing structure's
the cytoskeleton. We've inserted
microcapsules there with nano-sized pores.
The fabricated cells have inverted
destruction of your liver and, of course,
your pancreas. Looks like you might survive
despite yourself. Nanogenerators
keep the cells functioning so you can thrive.
They draw energy from blood flow. Take your
pills for another week to relieve pain,
then you're home free. No. You can't drink again.

Heart Exam

Watch the monitor. That small tissue mass
embedded in my right atrium: the
sinoatrial node, functioning as
a pacemaker. I'll magnify it. See
it quiver like a shaken kidney bean.
And its miniscule tear just under those
filaments. Yes, that's heartbreak—a slit lean
as an amoeba's membrane, but it throws
electric impulses out of kilter.
Would prove a killer, but it's securely
wrapped, tourniquet tight with minute strands clear
as gel. Sympathetic fibers? Surely.
Nanoscale guitar strings. A musician,
she somehow mended her own incision.

LOVING TO WATCH YOUR VOICE

You don't know this. I've linked my new spectrum
analyzer and Windows XP to
my phone. I gaze at your voice as you hum
then breathe your love song, sensual sotto
voce. Horizontal rippling rises
to full screen, creating dancing rainbows
in glistening waterfalls; disguises
your brief laugh as firefly confetti. Rows
of quivering colors flash then vanish
as you ask me what I'm feeling. Did you
know your phonemes' formants flow, so high-pitched,
twice as fast as mine—waveforms like bright blue
lightning? I'm recording this. You'll smile so
gently, viewing the e-mail video.

We and the Amoeba

Look in my microscope. I've magnified
a salt-water droplet, isolating
this single amoeba. Watch how it slides
on liquid pseudopods, hesitating,
quivering, then blink-quick the one cell splits
into twins. See their fluid shapes alter,
rapid as breath. Early naturalists
titled their genus *proteus* after
the Greek sea god with transforming body.
This process resembles our love—the way
we curl and slip, flexing torsos. But the
poignant reverse to protozoa: They
originate as one room, then divide.
Our lone souls unite when passions collide.

Post-Human

I sail over the Grand Canyon, eyeing
the Colorado's curled, staggered shore, its
titian hue, my spread-armed body flying
past scooped-toffee mountain walls. My hand hits
a buttress, rocks my balance, spins me down
toward water, my flipping gaze catching blurred
frames of distant hills tinted reddish brown,
like rare roast beef. Rapids magnify, stirred
to anger as I hurtle to them. Then
I stop me. My simulated me. Ease
me down, toes touching waves, hear cheering when
I begin to walk upstream, create trees
along the shoreline, sense my real me shout,
"Hell, the battery's died!" My light goes out.

OSTEOPOROSIS

The monitor shows your MRI scan.
See this magnified cross section of your
leg bone's outer layer, curving like an
off-white, pearl-handle casing, its inner
space filled with grains the color of fine malt?
That hidden stratum is spongy, lightweight
like inside a pillow, yet strong. The fault
lies in the center: these ebony, slight
ragged tears are growing, porous spaces
weakening the bone, as if termites were
hollowing a baseball bat. Some cases
show older white women suffer fractures
while ballroom dancing. Why? The sad factor:
Caucasian females lose bone mass faster.

PLACENTA

This bloody tissue prone in a small, blue
surgeon's tub appears a flattened eggplant
or enlarged purple heart the span of two
hands. Perhaps a wine-soaked palm leaf merchants
offer desert travelers in Egypt.
I'm half in shock—having witnessed my wife
bear our Bess, just swept to the well-equipped
incubator—and half enthralled at life
so fragile once secured by this organ,
ephemeral and now separated
from intimate touch of loving humans
who had shared its metabolism, fated
to be bound the rest of their lives. Doctor,
please save this for stem cells. Is that proper?

Brief Visit

I sit in semi-shade on the rain-worn
park bench near Canon Grill, the *Arkansas
Times* turned to Saban's story of greed-torn
historic homes and churches in free fall
throughout Helena's fragile neighborhoods.
Bradford pear trees above me surrender
to breeze, small white petals forming a flood
of pale confetti, swirling like winter
blizzard seen just last week in Manhattan.
One petal sticks to my hairy forearm.
Another settles on my folded hand.
Who could plan sharing such natural charms
as these, lying softly, curled like small shells,
then lifting away in wind's sudden swell?

Dinner at Diane's

Old farmhouse more than a pied-à-terre.
Her home. An aged depot, once docked
in Bigelow, its inner window here
still, frosted and marked "Tickets." We four walk
the pasture, breathe in the peace. Chris and I
then sit, catching up on years away, while
Renie grills lamb and Diane simmers sides
of spinach and cheese grits. We dine in style.
I must say this right now about love: you
really can find it at dinner tables
in candlelight, its flame reflected through
eyes of four old friends, focused gaze able
to channel deeper than you'll ever know.
There's more than moon, stars, candle here aglow.

OUR NIGHT, OUR AGE

for Mike and Cathy

From sensual bliss of pasta to soft
aphrodisiac of crumb cake, our night
flowed with consistency of easy love
as our nights seem to do, accepting plight
and pleasure as equal partners, our words
blending past and present like fine parfaits.
Back in my semi-Buddhist cell, I heard
some inner voice remind me of the way
age holds pain and hope gently, like small birds
with fragile wings, helping us pray to find
reason in Jerry Hum's act, or absurd,
lonely love notes, or Ryan in hot wind
of Iraq. Mostly age helps me perceive
how you two walk as one, love, laugh, and breathe.

Yellow Irises

A quartet with Kelly-green stalks standing
four feet high draw me off course from my walk
down Beechwood Street and into this sun-ringed
backyard to gaze like awe-struck lover, talk
softly as if wooing delicate blond
beauties posing for my camera, praise
their skin's silken texture as they respond
by shivering in breeze, each mid-rib braised
brown by some great Chinese artist's brushstroke
forming wing of a sleeping butterfly.
I lean close, whispering, "If you awoke
now to see me, would you lift to the sky,
carry fertile pollen to her garden,
surprise her with gifts of golden maidens?"

CRAPE MYRTLES

From a half block away, their light, brown-gray
trunks, slender as colts' legs, seem to shower
with green branches. Each limb's small bouquet sways
in the light breeze. Tuscarora flowers
of dark pink. Arapahoe glows bright red.
Lavender Muskogee and Natchez soft
white. Their explosions of color have spread
throughout Little Rock, filling enclosed crofts
of old homes, and stretches bordering streets
from the Heights to East Side. Nature's fine art
appears to have humbled July's harsh heat,
bartered brilliant hues for a later start
to summer's fire. How can I show how good
I feel, strolling my hometown neighborhoods?

Root Canal

for Jim Orahood

Nitrous flows from lungs to eyes, and I see
my late dad and mom smile. How gently they
hold one another. Under garden trees
lounge girls and women I've loved. Oh, I pray
for them all, silent phrases rising up
from the deep. And now prayers for this master
who I feel (pressure not pain) stir the cup
of my molar—hand sure as a cutter
of diamonds—focused on pulp's body:
arteries, veins, nerve fibers a figure
like some abstract Arc d'Triomphe. He frees
me of toxin, trigeminal's agony.
Post oxygen, I walk with humanity.

SUMMER

So, this late July day you've finally
come. Mother teased us for a month, smiling
and breathing soft, cool winds, rain storms barely
lasting an hour, leading lovers to sing
how spring always stays. Ah, we should have known
you were hiding under her apron, your
feet poised to leap out in surprise, blazed gown
spread like a wide-winged phoenix as you soar
around us in your torrid dance, fiery
kisses flowing from your lips. How they singe
each cheek and neck; hot vapors scorch every
nostril, lung and eye. No hope of revenge.
Mother's always liked you best, holds no pity
as you abuse dew point and humidity.

So You Want to Love a Poet

First, you can never trust her. When she says,
"I drown my kittens when they first open
their mouths," illusion of persona may
mask her. She wears colored contacts, hoping
you will never view true hue of her eyes.
She'll shove you with irony, knocking you
off balance to help find your center. Try
as you might, might proves worthless. Only true
self can save you. And her, too. Should you fall,
some unseen hand catches you. "Is this her?"
you may ask, but never know. Still, it all
depends on faith, I guess. When she whispers,
"I'm peeling off my flesh so you'll cover
me in yours," you pray you've found a lover.

Tattoo Regret?

Like a chorus line of pigmy wasps, this
Q-switched laser taunts my left forearm's skin.
Each blue letter of that name—Sweet Alice—
is slowly fading to a white blotch. When
the Village artist deeply ingrained her
in my dermis a decade ago, life
seemed a cloud. He was drunk; I was drunker.
Now the beauty Roxanne, my future wife,
shouts for Sweet Alice to vanish. It's far
from the sting of Sister Joan rapping palms
with a double-beveled ruler in our
younger days. All in all, I've stayed quite calm,
knowing Roxanne soon will face the wasp nest,
obliged to get ol' Rocky off her chest.

TANTRIC SEX?

I've cleansed my body head to toe, even
doubling the Neti pot's value, adding
salt to its warm water. Sandal paste's sheen
helps my physique glow, and offers padding
to my erotic scent. Pranayama
eases my Bhadrasana on the bed
as I prep for divine union's drama:
Gods Shiva and Shakti so subtly wed,
awakening the Sushumna Nadi,
arousing Kundalini from its coil,
climaxing in our Laja Samadhi.
What a celestial payment for my toil . . .
    This can't be right . . . I'm ripe for our mating . . .
    So why does she keep on meditating?

Second Life

I've had it with this bouncer's job, tossing
virtual muscle-bound creeps out of Club
Fondle, and owner Stud Wheeler bossing
me like I'm a Neanderthal for grub
and only 50 Linden dollars an
hour. Boobie Shaker, our best exotic
dancer, won't bed with me. She quit, began
a new gig as a banker. Think I'll stick
hands into real estate development.
Become a sleaze landlord . . . Wait a minute.
This Internet fantasy game was meant
to improve my real-world view. I've spent it
bogged down in my same lost-soul crap, only
scrapping my dreams. No wonder I'm lonely.

LUCAS AND BARNEY

Friday nights on Penn Station's concourse floor
Lucas walked with his imaginary
friend, the day's *Times* neatly folded and stored
in Lucas' back pocket, where he'd carry
it until Barney asked a question, or
flared out data Lucas couldn't believe.
He'd flick out the print gunfighter quick, flip
to the page, crease it, crutch it on his sleeve
to display for his bud, then swiftly slip
the proof back in its sheath, listen and leave
the talk to ol' Barn, a smile on his lips
of calm love, as if watching a sunrise,
his eyes tracking Barn's invisible eyes
in salute to his truth, his harmless lies.

The Island

She kept moaning of an island. "Palm trees
swarm it like green monsters," her voice whispered
over the cell phone. "It snows. The palms freeze."
I told her it can't snow where palms grow. Her
breath huffed like an adder. "Your palms freeze when
you touch my face." She was crying loud, fast,
in spasms. "I'm nearly there. Let me in
when I ring," I pleaded. "No. You swam past
the island. Nothing can save me now. Why
did you swim past?" The click shattered my ear.
I called her name. Only a void. When I
reached her place, I rang and shouted. Could hear
nothing inside. I kicked. Broke down the door.
Silence. The bathroom light. Blood on the floor.

Two Murders and a Suicide About to Happen

Mounted on the dull-yellow staircase wall
like unframed pictures: three violins—Alf,
Faruolo or Roubas perhaps. (Call
them Stradavarii if you want. They're half
the story anyway. Without them this
triangle would never have formed.) Their bows
of Pernambuco wood—dark cartharsis—
flow like tear trails, aimed toward the steps below.
Bordering the stringed trio, heavy masks
of drama and comedy in fine-carved
teak—their classic, still mouths seeming to ask
how three humans could become so love-starved.
Upstairs, the conductor husband discovers
two concert artists: his wife and her lover.

Virtual Immortality

Store this DVD in some cool, safe place.
Dr. Prime has recreated me—an
avatar so real, you'll swear my own face
(wrinkles too) laughs at your old jokes. I can
still mimic Johnny Cash to please you, botch
John Denver's high C and make you cringe. Prime's
melded AI and vidgame tech to such
a degree, he'll make the cover of *Time*.
He's caught my manners, moods, and most of all
memory. Still, you'll love controlling our
talks. You can make me stand silent, or call
me in to question, any day or hour.
3-D me can't kiss, but I can psych you
by whispering sweetly how I'd like to.

MITE HARVESTMAN

Before continental drift, Pangaea's
land mass resembled a slumped anteater
sitting on its rump. You housed areas
around the neck, front paw, posterior's
entire stretch. When The New World severed free
from West Africa, you were caught wading
near Miami; became stamped émigré
a hundred million years before Founding
Fathers and green cards. Now you hide out near
Tallahassee, under wet forest leaves
in Oregon and Washington. You veer
away from light, like timid monks or thieves,
a humble arachnid avoiding fame,
form small as the dot on "i" of your name.

The Romance of Amber

For her May birthday, I'll honor Roman
legend; offer her this amber necklace
encasing a tiny crocus. How can
I whisper in sensual tones and trace
this gemstone's history? Convert tree sap
to a lover caressing this fragile
flower? Reshape a poor blossom's mishap
into a bridal shower? I'm agile
as a centurion, in strong command
of amorous conversation. I'll show
why her jewel's lustrous globule demands
thirty million years to harden. And how
I impart this gift without reservation.
Ah! I'll use a PowerPoint presentation!

KUSH

On first hearing your name, we might perceive
easy jobs. Not so in your ancient land
straddling the Nile like a prone miner, sleeve
and pant legs burrowing in, his free hand
stretching toward Egypt. Your sun-burnished earth
holds a kingdom of relics: vast goldworks,
settlements, Merowe's pyramids worth
more to mankind than we'll ever know. Weirs
soon will flood you, displacing native tribes
with a hundred-mile lake. You know, progress.
Archeologists, researchers and scribes,
meanwhile, salvage ruins under duress
as dam builders prep electricity,
always of more value than history.

GRAPE CLUSTERS

These grape clusters clinging to vineyard limbs,
cresting and flowing out like sea-green founts,
form dark, mauve-shaded hearts, their outer rims
bulbous at top, narrowing to curled points
at base. Leaning my ear to dew-glistened
pericarps, I try godlike to fathom
these night-purple concords. If I listen,
perhaps I'll sense their deep-seeded rhythms
carried up from the earth. Maybe then I'll
absorb the pulse of healing origins:
how resveratrol aids my blood vessels
while cancers fall victim to psoralen.
I've read research papers of scientists.
Yet these vineyards enfold fertile secrets.

Viewing a Photosynthetic Photo

Yes, they look like honeycombs stuffed with green
peas, but they're plant cells holding chloroplasts:
biological pathway's pavement, means
for keeping us alive. Your salad's last
romaine leaf, there on your fork—organelles
galore. We heterotrophs thrive on such
veggies, breathing oxygen they expel,
then ripping laminae from earth to munch
the mesophyll jazzed up with vinegar
and oil. Light energy turning to
chemical power within us—the star
of our existence. When our lunch is through,
let's speak of our declining aquifers,
since this whole life process requires water.

FLIGHT OF THE BEES

In July, researchers in the UK
and Netherlands revealed how they've vanished,
colony hives fallen eighty fold. Look
where you will, Andrena gravida's wish
seems not to be seen, leaving apple trees
bare, cherries a faint dream, dandelions
only memory in fields outside Leeds,
tulips fading like melting snow in and
beyond Amsterdam's vast gardens. And now
America senses droneless silence
in California valleys, still meadows
of once florid Georgia, where swarms so dense
turned noon into night. The old farmer sighs,
listens for lost sounds, whispers to the skies.

THE LARK DESCENDING

See that porch's gaslight? Its flame flickers
smaller and smaller as fuel fades away.
That's us slowly dying. Yes. You snicker.
Feel I mean just you and me. Did you say,
after reading "Flight of the Bees," "Oh, they'll
come back?" Shall I cite Audubon's harrowed
report? Twenty common bird species fell
70 fold in 40 years. Sparrow,
bobwhite, meadowlark . . . Shall I go on? No?
Let's argue how humans encroach, adapt,
and expect smaller lives to ride our low
conveyor belt of change. Well, the belt's snapped.
Can we fix it for our children, knowing
our limits? Let's . . . Wait! Where are you going?

The Last Place

He determined his human race undone.
Read in Nostradamus how Ibiza's
prevailing winds would shun Armageddon.
Sailed through Mediterranean breezes
to that island shaped like a floating frog.
Landed a mountain farm caressed by high
pine forests, his home of petrified logs
and ancient Phoenician stone nurtured by
a clear spring singing twenty feet away
from his door. No computer. No TV.
No radio. No CD. Thin pine's sway,
cricket's and pipit's calls his reverie,
he views stars, far lights of Vila's center,
no longer fearing nuclear winter.

Strumpets

What shall we do to get the vote? Spread our
political legs to left and right, that
way covering the center? Scorn power
while holding secret meetings in our flats
to plan moves for taking control? Leer to
shaft the public, insure ignorance, pick
their pockets while they sleep? Shouldn't we do
them in by causing wars, assure they're sick
through poison air, water, food, twisted words
of race, class, nation and creed? Condemn greed
while taking corporate kickbacks? You heard
our pimps laughing, didn't you? When they read
their poll results, they know citizens scoff,
feel we screw them. But we're just beating off.

SNIPER PRODIGY

The preteen boy steadies his M40
rifle, clear blue eye centering distant
target—a Vietcong bivouac's sentry
fifty meters away—in an instant
through his telescopic sight. Calculates
minute of angle to assure he'll rip
the skull. Wishes he could insure such fate
for Jenny Warner's boyfriend as he flips
the trigger. Feels blood's hot rush—his first kill
of the day. He hunts this way after school
each weekday for hours . . . Hears a sound . . . grows still.
Someone's in the hallway. He plays it cool,
eyes fixed on the screen. Hears his mom exclaim
to friends, "He loves his new video game!"

THE ARMCHAIR ASSASSIN

This satellite view of Concepción
Volcano on my monitor appears
a cadaver's brown, shriveled breast, caught on
fire deep within, smoke pouring from vast tears
in its nipple. We start to see lahars,
like molten concrete, cover villages
below, turning them to smoldering stars.
See that first one? Ortega's entourage
is there, I guess. Or one just to the left,
depending on whether they stopped to eat
lunch. Our cruise missle's nuclear head kept
the faith, a bull's-eye in the crater's seat.
Too bad we lost so many innocents.
Don't ask the amount of money we spent.

The Armchair Assassin II

Terra satellite shows the Caspian,
my old friend, black as thick oil beneath it.
But I must focus now on this crimson
speck by Turkmenistan's shore. Rebels hit
an oil derrick west of Halliburton's
marine base. In a jiff I'll home in tight
on the chalk-brown earth beneath thin curtains
of clouds, measure my laser's pinpoint sight,
hook up with those secret jets just off shore.
Missiles will blast rebs like our Afghan strike
in '98 that shut Taliban's door
to a pipeline. Soon we'll fire away like
clockwork—when we get the call—at Iran,
making lava of its nuclear plants.

The Armchair Assassin III

Last night in Topeka, Rosa's Tex-Mex
tasted like chateaubriand compared to
this stale-bread ham here at Forbes. Torrid sex
'til dawn with Ginnie, then needing to screw
now with this Dell, can't compare. Here I am,
activated again from Arkansas,
controlling this Predator drone—its cam
eyeing an Al Farouq factory's haul
outside Kandahar—prepping to propel
four Hellfires, burning building and work crews
to cinders. I once threw paper missiles
in Father Groff's history class. One flew
harmlessly hitting the back of his head.
A long way from fathers I now leave dead.

The Armchair Assassin IV

We didn't mind when they murdered within
their own borders, like Politkovskaya's
shooting in an elevator, ricin
bloating Shchekochikhin's lungs with mire as
he breathed. But Litvinenko's poisoning
with polonium—some careless agent
spreading its alpha radiation in
London's parks and eateries—rips the tent.
My Terra satellite's spy lens hovers
over Putin's Kremlin pad. The clock ticks.
His Labrador, Koni, its teeth covered
with tiny capsules of sarin, will nick
Vlady's hand like always. I'll know he dived
fast once I see the ambulance arrive.

THE AESTHETIC ASTRONAUT

THE ARMCHAIR ASSASSIN V

I've waited to hammer this scum since they
took our guys hostage in '79
with Carter flat on his ass. Bergner says
Quds now arm Iraqi insurgents. Fine.
Just watch me please the Chief and blast them to
crisp wafers of flesh, turn silos to ash.
Advanced Crystal/IKON provides stark views
of the Saghand mine huge as the deep gash
on my girlfriend's face. The Ardekan nuke
fuel unit's so sharp, I can almost taste
the yellowcake. By dusk, missiles will juke
all twelve weapon sites. We'll then track and waste—
to aid the Company—ayatollahs.
By noon, they'll wish they'd never canned the Shah.

The Armchair Assassin VI

I'm reading Cheney's Halliburton rap
from '98: How Caspian oil
should flow through Afghanistan. As I tap
the sat's lens on Qandahar to spoil
any assaults on a pipeline, the call
comes in. Putin's pulled from the CFE.
Plus he won't jerk troops from Georgia. I stall
one cam's orbit, focus on Tbilisi,
a key to the BTC line. This shit's
about to get serious. But that's why
I lob missiles: secure oil profits.
The Chief cell-phoned me today. "Don't be shy,"
he said, "about protecting my buddies."
I'll melt those Russkies to silly putty.

The Armchair Assassin VII

To help you assist me, I will explain
why we're here: In '72, Saddam
nationalized the oil, forcing our main
U.S. and U.K. firms out. Then the damn
devil's son let the Frogs, Russkies and Chinks
move in. We turned that when we invaded,
then made sure the new constitution links
Iraq's oil with our guys. We've evaded . . .
the Chief I mean . . . this in his press confabs.
No one knows about us. Those monitors
on the right keep 24/7 tabs
on 70 fields from Gusair to Noor.
Still, our global satellites cover all.
And we're prepped to kill when we get the call.

The Armchair Assassin VIII—Upheaval Dome

Our space station's over the Canyonlands
National Park. See that deep cavity
circled by jagged cliff slopes like a tanned,
coiled snake? We theorize gravity
sucked in a meteor 60 million
years back. Chinle and Moenkopi sandstone
at center create, from here, illusions
of gray-green and white-foam rapids dashed on
island rocks and lashing vast red crags. But
it's all sand-based solids. We'll start dropping
Guantanamo detainees at night; put
a few from secret Company camps. Bring
in trained Dobermans to engage in sport.
We'll teach those guys to challenge us in court.

The Armchair Assassin IX

Official word says we ashed Bosnia's
6,000 MANPADS three years ago. But
now the Company negates that. Some ass
sold 200 to bin Laden who shut
them tight in Tora Bora. He's set to
share the wealth with terrorist cells worldwide.
I just got coordinates on the two
White Mountain caves where Osama's guards hide
the missiles. Those hills look like some GI
bunked under a wrinkled army blanket.
They house former outposts built by our guys
for Muslims to fight the Russkies. I bet
you'll just see piles of rubble when we're done.
They should have let me blast him in '01.

THE ARMCHAIR ASSASSIN X

I'm not much good for attacking our own,
but orders are orders. American
farmers, pissed as hell at wetback crackdowns,
have amassed land inside Mexico and
Central America. The Chief said sear
that offshore crap. Our satellite lenses
trail those gliders easily through the clear
night skies of Baja and Belize. Rinses
of maltoxin will damage lettuce crops
and paralyze crews who work tomorrow.
Our sucker punch under stars puts a stop
to their harvests. You could hear the Chief crow.
I asked if our strikes caused market downturns.
His glare made real clear that's not our concern.

The Armchair Assassin XI

My IKON has ID'd the Chink website's
hideout right inside Nanjing. Titan Rain's
cyberhacked the Pentagon's once air-tight
classified networks. They've become a pain
now, tapping in to our high-tech command
shop at Barksdale. I've hawked the Company's
minisub night mission, gliding as planned
from the East China Sea up the Yangtze.
The target's less than 50 yards away
from the piers. One SRBM should scrap
the whole neighborhood. Just ruin their day.
Waste maybe a thou. Ching-chong brass will crap.
I hope they push us. We'll show who's faster,
turning Peijing into melted plaster.

THE ARMCHAIR ASSASSIN XII

I'm monitoring Company agents
interrogating this Qaeda suspect.
Amazing his head's unbruised from the stint
of slaps with a rolled phone book. You'd expect
that assault and the ripped-out fingernails
to be called torture. But Justice says no.
Or stripping him naked, feet in ice pails—
his unheated cell able to store snow—
blindfolded, pushed backward on a flat board,
flooding his gagged mouth and nose with water.
Makes him feel he's suffocating. A hoard
of heavy metal CDs will batter
his eardrums for five straight hours. We'll bare,
not what he knows, but what we want to hear.

Waterboarding Cats

It's tougher than with humans, he tells me.
Can't tie their arms behind them, so their claws
cause problems sometimes. Still, they look funny,
strapped belly-up on the board, layered gauze
masks he soaks with water each five minutes,
gagging, hacking, spewing, screeching in plumed
spurts when their gurgling throats catch breath, send it
spraying out in gasps like mist from perfume
bottles. Thin legs flail. Thrashing paws slash down
at air like curved, starved bird beaks. He feels bad
sometimes, he says, if he errs, a cat drowns
or suddenly snaps inside, going mad.
"They're not like humans, you know—evil men
who'll lie to you, kill for their religion."

THE AESTHETIC ASTRONAUT

Hello, Houston. Do you see Envisat's
radar image as I do? These massive
South Asia flooded regions imitate
delicate royal-blue gowns, starlit sleeves
to rival Klimt's portrait of Emilie
Floge. Yes, those speckled patterns of dry land
among erupting waters. One could be
an ornate slipper toeing the curled bands
of the Ganges and Brahmaputra. Look
how both Calcutta and Dhaka pose as
sculpted snowdrifts—portraits from Rosing's book
of polar landscapes . . . Anyhow . . . Best pass
word to response teams: Urgent you secure
weak levees near Pabna and Jamalpur.

THE AESTHETIC ASTRONAUT II

See north of Athens, that area stained
like unpolished amethyst, its curling
body a drowsy dragon yawning. Rain
turned it that color, halted the hurling
flames. They devoured some four thousand acres
of Mount Parnitha's firs and pines, once deep
emerald, like the flowing forest cape
surrounding the serpent. Cinders in steep
crevices still glow like snakes' eyes at night,
but lie far from dry wood and pose no threat.
Karavola, the summit, felt the plight
of smoke and ashen air, but no fire. Let
me site the Acropolis: Socrates'
southern gray mass seeming piled like crushed slate.

The Aesthetic Astronaut III

Houston, this cluster of frost deposits
sweeping across Ontario's coast gleam
like a Tiffany bracelet on the wrist
of a Cree maiden, her skin of dark cream
matching Akimiski's crescent, as well
as nearby Charlton Island, which appears
a heifer-head broach. Further north's a swell
of swirling white winter sea ice like tiers
of melting opals caught on canvas by
Pollack. That's Polar Bear Provincial Park,
on James Bay's western coast. I don't know why,
but northern ice is breaking up, a stark
contrast to previous springs with a lone
white mass of land and seascape, like scraped bone.

The Aesthetic Astronaut IV

I wish I'd never caught this shuttle view
of the Small Magellanic Cloud—millions
of stars, red dwarfs to supernovas, hues
so rich they vie with rainbows, their bullions
of acrylic light blazing, hydrogen
gas and dust swirling in stellar winds. It's
not their massive constellation open
like some giant, flaming cavity that
stuns me; but that single burst of sky-blue
cloud, burning bright as her clear eye's iris.
Houston, I know regs ban saying this to
you, but I must tell someone how I miss
her. This black hole inside me is a curse.
Please, just let me scream to the universe.

The Aesthetic Astronaut V

I know we label Mars the Red ·Planet,
but, Houston, this mosaic of Valles
Marineris's hemisphere befits
mirror image for Gorgonzola cheese,
swirls and splotches of blue marble engrained
in vast, creamy terrain. I'm looking down
on Olympus Mons now. This massive, stained
mount dwarfs our Mauna Loa. Its huge brown
cliffs seem an irate monkey's furry face,
vast caldera its screaming mouth, a pair
of collapsed craters as glaring eyes. Trace
its ashen-toned escarpment that appears
a stained silver frame, it turns a trophy
lying on some thick, boundless flokati.

Yeah, I knew two of 'em. Harry real well.
On his second tour. Found him lyin' near
Baghdad on a dune. His skull blown to hell.
Put his SAW in his mouth, flicked the trigger.
That little Janie they shipped to Kabul?
Said she was bipolar. Aped ol' Harry,
but in her bunk. Man, those blue eyes could pull
you to her like shortcake to strawberries.
'member West, red curly hair? Tried to glug
booze and a bag of sleepin' meds. Barfed 'em
up. Scooter wrote me. His Guard unit dug
out of the Sunni Triangle for home.
Slit his wrists in his den. PTSD.
Naw, he pulled through. Shit. Should've let him bleed.

My Government-Censored Sonnet

Sitting here in Guantanamo's dark █,
I hear the guard shout, "█████!" through my cell
window, high above █████'s pristine vale.
In that room down the hall, prisoners █,
███, and ██ like children from the ████. █████.
What have I done to deserve this? Loud calls
from interrogators █████ to cure
our silence. One voice ████, "I'll cut your ████
off if you don't ████!" What to say when my
time comes? Tell them how my wife ████ wonders
where I ██, if I'm still ███? Ask why
I'm here? Request evidence they ████
then will present █████ me? All I know
is they offer no █████, only shadows.

THE PHONE CONVERSATION

"Hello, Ann. It's Ed." *"Hi, Ed."* "When I come
over tonight, should I bring condoms?" *"Well,
I think it's a little soon . . ."* **"Take condoms!
You want to be secure!"** "Hey, who the hell's
listening in to our conversation!?!"
**"I'm with the National Security
Agency. We've been tapping both your phones
for a year."** *"Damn! I'll call AT&T!"*
**"Don't bother. We're partners. We want you to
be secure. Including with sex. So use
condoms."** "I thought you just tapped people who
are terrorists. Government can't abuse
an average American like me!"
"Teehee . . . You've been watching too much TV."

Homeless

I get mixed up sometimes. Not sure if I'm
defending my worn mattress under this
train bridge near the state capitol's prime
parking spaces, or still prepping to diss
some gook attacking our overpass near
Pleiku. The fog usually covers me
at night when I start to drift off. Cape Fear,
I call it. Or, worse, when I'm suddenly
startled awake by movement nearby. I
nearly killed old Cedric last week. Wined out,
he stumbled and fell into me. As my
hand cocked to crumple his neck, Nick shouted
my name and grabbed me. He served in Iraq.
Tonight we'll watch stars through bridge spans. Smoke crack.

A Short History of the CIA

The day after I turn four, my country
(the government that is) okays the sneaks
in overcoats, their covert gallantry
spiced by zapping foreign leaders. Blank checks
help set up coups, while Project Bluebird rigs
mind control as my candles burn seven.
My last year in high school, the Bay of Pigs
sends Company heads rolling. Eleven
summers post, McCord et al blow the break
at Watergate, prompting Congress to don
spyglasses. I'm forty-four, the Hill takes
on Iran-Contra. Will the sneaks be gone?
When I'm fifty-eight, they're back in power
as mad Muslims fell New York's twin towers.

FREE TIBET

Kansas City winter night, my daughter
sits knitting a wool scarf for her business,
softly singing of Tibetans slaughtered
in Lhasa, of their artisans impressed
into textile mills, of a nun dying
in Drapchi Prison just last month. She leans
her head back, eyes closed, now nearly crying,
voice almost a whisper while revealing
the reprise: "Free Tibet, oh, free Tibet."
Knitting needles pause in their nodding dance.
Her hands raise the scarf, study wool ringlets
for any flaw. Then her earth-deep eyes glance
at me. "What would you do," they seem to say,
"if soldiers came here and took me away?"

Homeless II

The spotted owl—folded wings like an air
photo of a deep-brown, craggy mountain
etched with snow packs—rests on the white oak's bare
branch above the sloped bank of Oregon's
Wolf Creek. Moonlight through clouds sets it center
stage. Native westerner, its nest's fallen
prey to the barred owl, eastern invader
named for its long, feathered beard, a frozen
waterfall striped its length with dried blood streaks.
Headlights flash over the near hill, swiping
the spotted. Its beak spreads like talons, shrieks
as, like glistening war bonnets, its wings
spread, lift swift as a thought through the night sky.
Logging trucks park at the new mill nearby.

We Say Goodbye to the Dying

I stand at this hospital bed watching
a once lovely woman, body shriveled
by leukemia, her worn lungs catching
air in staggered lunges, hair disheveled
by bands from her oxygen mask. She sleeps
that sleep of the dying, tense and labored.
Years ago, I studied my mother, deep
in her rasping coma. How she savored,
though unconscious, our moistening her dry
lips with wet cotton, soothing her forehead
with warm cloth and kisses. We say goodbye
to the dying, not knowing what's ahead,
with tones of hope. Then gaze in mute surprise
when, in that final breath, their spirits rise.

BIRTH OF A SUPERNOVA

This gigantic star I magnify through
ESO's telescope seems a frosted
tangerine flashbulb igniting. Gas flue
at its base feeds that White Dwarf's disk—rust red,
bright as creation, warped glow recalling
the eye of God. Its trembling mass ignites.
Flamed gases flower, swirled clouds unveiling
a vast, orange-white carnation of light
greater than our sun. Ah, please say hello
to the supernova, heaven's brilliant
young artist, its expanding inferno
near-perfect foil for black holes' indignant
desire to devour stars. Can it be so?
This passionate fire blazed light years ago?

Mother Star

And now we know about inspiration,
how it explodes from inside us just like
this Cone Nebula's massive gyration
ignites these smaller sun-like stars: a strike
of some magnificent celestial match
sending light years of phosphorus spheres through
swirls of space. From our home on earth, we watch
this gallant galactic shower. Its hues
and blaze remind us how the loving Muse
smiles when we kneel to her, breathes gently on
our candle's flame, inviting us to use
this swelling glow around us and deep down
within. In the heavens, the light expands.
We feel its fire within our hearts and hands.

PRAYER

Since every sense is prayer, know when I think
of you, image forms communion with All.
My astral telescope's focus, succinct
as flame, holds this great nebula's starfall
and sees you there. My streaming Internet
captures Vaughn Williams' "The Lark Ascending."
I hear you in its violin. Forget
your warm breast against mine? I'm pretending
you lie here now. Velvet taste of sweet cream
atop my latte recalls your lip gloss.
Light jasmine perfume flowing through my dream
hints of you in the room. Since every loss
is prayer, I praise what others call a curse,
sending out this song to the universe.

George Tribou

Years later, as the great priest lay in deep coma,
light of St. Vincent's private room dimming
as it must, result of cancer's trauma,
Mike sat at his bedside. Remembering
how the monsignor liked John Knowles, Mike read
from *A Separate Peace*, hoping spoken
rhythms flowed, easing journey to sacred
space where body cannot go. Leg broken,
denying war, Finney recovered while
Gene wallowed in guilt. Pausing for respite,
Mike watched our mentor sleep, then whispered, "I'll
stop. Guess you're tired as I of hearing it."
The old man barely shook his head "no" twice.
A teacher's bit of last loving advice.

BILL CLARK

September 9, 1943–May 15, 2007

Long before he got his degree, Bill Clark
would lift off the swimming pool's concrete court
those summers at War Memorial Park,
proving through basketball's electric sport
he'd already mastered engineering.
The sphere would slip smoothly from his two hands
through the rim's metal net; left me cheering
or scowling, whatever the score. He'd stand
laughing, calling, "Man, you'll never stop me!"
No one ever did, really. He dashed on
to finish college, married a beauty,
built family, business, reputation,
not missing a shot throughout the long game.
I still smile every time I hear his name.

CASH'S LAST CALL

Riding Saturday in her small station
wagon, my old friend Diane plays Johnny
Cash's fifth "America" CD: one
last call for love. I give thanks it's sunny
as his voice—falling to cruel assaults
from asthma and pneumonia—rasps, quivers,
calm and resigned. His phlegm-scarred throat may halt
full, pure lines. Yet, just as ancient rivers
stubbornly flow, so does the Man in Black.
He's worn out, sad, at times even breathless.
Still, his tone and words can carry us back
to younger days: our hearts strong and restless.
We listen, silent. He sings of a ghost
to someone—that woman he still loves most.

WARRIOR BRINGING PEACE

for Major Tim Williams

In 1919, history books tell
us, under Amanullah Kahn, the Third
Anglo-Afghan War began. Now we've heard
how a warlord of similar name fell
last November. And now how you, no way
to tell the future, went down from Shindand
to Zerco Valley, hope in heart, to say,
"Let us have peace here." And how warlords' hands
clasped in concord, exchanged Holy Korans,
silencing screams of death between the tribes.
And now you stand in green robe with gold strands,
gold medal over your heart, words inscribed
to honor your bringing peace, your blue eyes
looking somewhere. Perhaps home: the great prize.

George Orwell

Years before talking animals and Thought
Police, you stood in the trench near Huesca,
dawn at your back, when the Fascist's gunshot
bolted through the air, tunneling your neck.
Sandbags shrunk to teabags as your eyes glazed,
blood seeping from your lips. The glaring streaks
of light fused with spewed gasps. Mates' whispers phased
to sloshing footsteps bearing you as squeaks
of your stretcher recalled a child's new shoes.
Somehow that image assured you of life.
A silver poplar leaf brushed your eyebrow,
making you long for Eileen, your new wife.
She would join you soon, caring for the wound.
You'd heal, your voice a haunting, muted sound.

GERALD STERN

Jack just e-mailed a poem by Gerald
Stern, Pittsburgh boy, citing Galileo's
metaphor for the mind: paper scrap hurled
by wind. Anxious squirrel threatened by throes
of truck wheels, Stern says, best fits his writer's
psychic reality. I saw him read
once in the '80s—night of harsh winter
on the Jersey Shore—and began to heed
how poets prep us for the kill. Bald, plump,
grandfather's serene smile, he lured us toward
false security with baggy frame slumped
at the lectern. Then the hiding leopard
leapt from the dark, slashed minds with craft-sure claws
of piercing phrases, stroked hearts with his paws.

Hitler

History says Adolph, Old High German
for noble wolf (called "my Uncle Wolf" by
Winifred Wagner), held Eva Braun's hand
as he blew his brains out, taking a bite
of cyanide for insurance. Eva
aped him, arm cuffed by her favorite gold
bracelet with the green stone. Not all believe
it. Phil feels they copped a mansion: some old
estate in Brazil. Lois finds their niche
somewhere high in the Himalayas. I
swear I see him once a week in Greenwich
Village, withered, limping, with wild blue eyes,
shouting through wolf teeth (spewing his sandwich)
he's been robbed by the corner deli's Jews
or the old black man who just shined his shoes.

HYPATIA

What flashed through your mind—its insight revered
by men like Socrates Scholasticus—
when the Christian mob, mad with zeal, murdered
you with tiles after stripping your carcass?
Did decades of teaching math help you gauge
brutal wrath of the body politic?
In the Caesareum, religious rage
swarming, did Aristotle's "Poetics"
help you cope? Nope? After sharp potshards scraped
your flesh clean from mangled limbs they burned near
Cinaron, John of Nikiu's writings shaped
you as witch. Did your spirit slough his smear,
praying for foul, desperate flocks who condemn
women from Alexandria to Salem?

I'VE SEEN GREAT MEN FROM A DISTANCE

The Styrofoam coffee cup echoing
across the concrete like some haywire clock
invites me to trail its staggered blowing
down Kavanaugh. I follow for a block
and a half until it halts beneath some
blue SUV parked outside of Leo's
gyro shop. Suddenly memory comes
sweeping back: My literary hero
Kurt Vonnegut strolling outside of Grand
Central Station in 1989.
How I decided to linger, then blend
in with the shadows as I trailed behind
perhaps thirty feet, matching his calm gait,
catching up when stoplights forced him to wait

at each corner of 42nd Street.
Cordovan loafers, brown slacks, tweed jacket,
right hand holding an umbrella he'd treat
like a walking cane, his steel-gray packet
of curly hair and thick mustache encased
a face serene as his pace. No social
critic this day. His eyes glowed, seemed erased
of any feeling except love for all
the great city displayed. At last I left
him outside the Main Library as he
rose past its silent lions to well-kept
volumes tracing our hope and doom. We're free
thanks to words like his, urging us to seek
our own words. So he lived. He died last week.

James Meredith

Freedom to change has proved your battle call.
You filed suit to attend Ole Miss—its first
black student and graduate. Saw two fall
dead in riots as you entered. Were cursed
in and after classes 'til they handed
you the diploma. Caught a sniper's slug
on your peace walk to Jackson. Abandoned
civil rights. Became a stockbroker. Shrugged
off your brave past to join Republicans.
Ran for the Senate and lost. Complain how
white liberals prevent a black's advance,
stifling growth with welfare programs. So now,
grown old breaking the hero's mold, you can
fade quietly like most Americans.

JEFFERSON AND THE DECLARATION

Your lyrical breadth still amazes me.
You melded your words with Lee, Franklin and
Adams, the Dutch Republic's stern decree,
phrases from Virginia's draft—even planned
to resolve slavery's end 'til the South
threatened our document's death. Still, your Muse
scalded the king with such scorn, every mouth
surely fell, hearing depths of his abuse.
McNair tacked up one of Dunlap's broadsides
in Independence Hall's courtyard, the first
reading outside Congress. Did you decide
alone to close your work with sacred verse?
Pledging lives, fortunes, honor, your voice rose.
Leaders today rasp in empty echoes.

John Gould Fletcher

Though Little Rock's library branch hails you,
it offered only one volume—*South Star*—
that day I sought your words. A native who
won poetry's Pulitzer, you're worth far
more. Wanderer, you proved Wolfe wrong, coming
home again. Fame had chased you from New York
to England where you refused succumbing
to Pound's editing; saw your free-verse work
in Imagist anthologies. Poets,
still, deeply sense roots—their churning life-flow;
hear the haunting rhythm of home; know it's
vital for honest writing, like sun's glow.
Yet bipolar disorder's bitter knife
carved slowly through; bled you of hope and life.

JOSEPH

for Ron Cassaday

Arrayed in your rainbow cloak, you explained
your brothers' dreams. They threw you in a pit.
Then you defined Pharaoh's vision, how grain
would flourish then fail; moved from jail to sit
as the king's viceroy. Worth a treasury
more than the 20 shekels which once sold
you into slavery, you found pleasure
in testing your brothers, cared for your old
father, changed Egypt's land-tenure system.
Now you shine in the torah, some Christians
honor a great saint, while faithful Muslims
see you as prophet, called "Moon of Canaan."
Yet my heart feels, despite all these dressings,
you still value most old Jacob's blessings.

Max Perkins

for Ted Parkhurst

Throughout each day, Max Perkins would edit
every phrase with no discretion. He'd
even flip words when tired. To his credit,
he remained faithful, sharing his small seed
with only one woman, and his slight swing
where they'd idle side by side, like bookends
awaiting hardbounds never arriving.
Did he label the publisher a friend?
Did his spirit rise high enough to love?
Bird watchers might know. And we can pretend
his preening proved a sign. He liked above
more than below, at least until the end,
when his floor circling announced the sad stroke,
and he fell silent, wrapped in pastel cloak.

MODIGLIANI

Your pen-and-ink nude of Akhmatova
worships her slender form, lithe curves of her
long arms. Your yearlong affair shaped a trove
for her poems. When you lashed as lovers,
volcanoes wakened, your artists' passions
firing new stars. She returned to marriage
and fame: Dubbed "Anna of all the Russias"
at 23. In Paris, disparaged
by debt, booze, and TB, you never stopped
painting with fire, portraying mistresses,
friends with almond-shaped heads, affixed atop
narrow necks like stretched stumps of stripped birches.
Meninges ablaze, you burned up inside,
only 35 and broke when you died.

PADRE PIO

Your photo portrays arms gently crossed, hands
bearing wounds like large bullet holes above
the wrists. Shy, you covered them with dark bands
when you said Mass. Shocked, the Holy See shoved
you from the confessional, denied your
demonic fistfights, your bilocating
to help souls at risk, the rose-rich odor
often flowing from you. The church's sting
eased as Pope Pius privately confessed
he'd been "badly informed." Still, you lived long
and died in Italy's ankle; professed
how we should "Pray, hope and don't worry!" Throngs
flocked to your funeral. Many still pray
to St. Pio of Pietrelcina.

Sylvia and Ted

She had almost seduced him to forsake
Assia, move back with her and the kids
to Devon, like the old days. Hoped to make
their passion return, screwing him amid
creaks of the gray tweed couch. But he left her
in the second-floor flat at 23
Fitzroy Road, the house where Yeats once lived. Where
she set out fresh bread and milk for Frieda
and Nicholas, sealed their closed room with wet
cloths and towels, then shoved her head inside
the gas-flowing oven. Ted would regret
this and more: Assia's own suicide
after killing their child. Meanwhile, swirls of snow
lashed like ripped pages at Sylvia's window.

Swan

for Priscilla

Centered near the top of your delicate
stationery, it seems to float at ease,
resting between flowing letters that state
your first and last name, its image released
and multiplied on your dining table,
with eight porcelain sisters caressing
two small oranges. Their smooth beaks able
to lie on their breasts like soft hands resting
in prayer or sleep, they may be gleaning
hints of hymns rising from their sibling who
nests near your bathroom sink. While it's preening
its pewter feathers, glass wings seem set to
glide out toward some silver lake far away,
creating legend leading to ballet.

TESLA

Unlike foe Edison, who trudged through dogged
study, you divined grand inventions in
fully constructed visions. Teachers dodged
your genius, would accuse you of cheating
for solving calculus problems in your
head. At 24, you foresaw AC
currents propelling induction motors
as you recited Goethe. Poetry,
then, would shake science. Your great idea
would change lives, lead to electric power
grids, stun thousands at Chicago's fair—a
"City of Light"—soon see its glow shower
the globe. Years later, dead of heart failure,
the feds tried to steal your private papers.

The Frost Place

Your half-decade here—"the Franconia
years"—bonded depths of pain with growing fame.
Fresh from England, shouldering praise and a
pair of first books, you let Henry Holt claim
you; sought and purchased this farm and small home,
porch framing the White Mountains. Elinor
miscarried. Word came of Edward. You'd roam
the woods, grieve, collect plants, let rhythms pour
into you, mold them to verse while rocking
slowly at your cluttered desk. The kids played.
Elinor weaved wit and silence, locking
you in and out, and you her. Still, you stayed
linked like root and earth; held close through tremors
from love's madness, death, your great lion's roar.

THE IMPRESSIONIST

Artwork flows from my old friend Ted as though
he's years behind or hasn't much time. I
suppose we're all there, feeling our breath blow
from us like a last flight, then empty sky.
I keep thinking of his pastel landscape:
green sea grass stretching to unseen ocean,
distant old post rising from among blades,
a still oriole atop, no notion
of flying away. Can't stop wondering
about that post: Cracked fragment of a pier
on a now-receded shore? Stilt daring
to support a house now lost? Brace for tiers
to view boats long gone? Whatever I see,
as all artists do, he leaves that to me.

Archangel Gabriel and I

are drinking our coffees in Starbucks when
I state, "Let me get this straight: Christians say
you informed Mary she'd bear Jesus, then
broke the news to Joseph." Sipping latte,
he winks yes. "Jews preach you told Noah to
build the ark, and kept young Isaac alive.
You even placed Moses inside his tomb."
Licking whipped cream, he nods affirmative.
"Muslims believe you revealed the Koran
to Muhammad, stood with him to assist
his ascension. Why can't you help humans
see horrors of war and make them desist?"
He flaps a wing, shrugs, takes my two bread sticks,
munches, leans close, and whispers: "Politics."

JUNG AND I

lounge in his dim study. At last shuffling
and dealing old Tarot cards, he wheezes
a whisper: "Turn one over." I'm scuffling
with myself to choose. He smoothly eases
one toward me, watching my eyes. I flip it:
a naked young woman rides a seven-
headed lion. "Lust." The murmured snippet
rises from behind me. It's Freud. "Heavens
no," Jung snaps back. "The card symbolizes
courage, inner strength. See the Holy Grail?"
"Oedipus complex," Sigmund grunts, rises,
stalks from the room. "He does this without fail,"
Carl sighs. He checks his watch, lifts his teacup.
"I'd cite deeper meanings, but your hour's up."

HAYDEN AND I

are walking in Greenwich Village, and I'm
wearing my Sony Walkman; he's sporting
his powdered wig, recalling when he climbed
a wall to see the empress cavorting
in Vienna's court. "I was only twelve,"
he chuckles. But I can't hear him because
the volume from my earphones only shelves
any chance I have. Still, I sense him pause
in his stride. I look up and watch him frown
like a teacher seeing a pupil sleep.
I know my buddy feels I've let him down.
I hand him my earphones: "Here, yours to keep."
He slips them over his wig . . . Eyes grow wild.
I know he hears *Die Schopfung*. And he smiles.

Picasso and I

saunter through the Arkansas Arts Center's
galleries. We reach Pablo's surreal "Still
Life with Red Bull's Head." Black magic marker
in hand, he steps over the knee-high rail,
studies the bull's crooked eyes, one Cyclops-
centered, one near its left ear. The legend
glares, darkening each night-fading iris.
A female guard tackles the Spaniard, sends
him to the floor. "You crazy old fart!" she
screams. "You're destroying art!" "He's enhancing
his work," I retort. "It's Picasso. See."
She smiles in surprise. They begin dancing.
Fondling her blue blazer, the master leers:
"Ever made love with an old man, my dear?"

The U.S. Supreme Court and I

are mingling over whiskeys in Roberts'
chambers, quintet majority giggling
about trashing our civil liberties,
the minority judges bent wriggling
in despair. "We goosed that Alaskan kid
daring to display his sign off campus!"
the rookie Alito laughs. "Screwed the lid
on taxpayers exposing the White House
for its marrying church and state!" guffaws
Scalia. "And corporate and union
bosses now can pick presidents!" heehaws
Thomas. "What about the Constitution?"
I butt in. "You know . . . The First Amendment?"
The chief justice growls, "Damn all precedents!"

WILLIAM JAMES AND I

sally along Broadway near Astor House,
his birthplace. He suddenly starts to whirl—
pirouette flows to soft-shoe. He's aroused
my prying: "Does this unexpected twirl
arise from some concrete spiritual
experience?" He smiles as he spins past
me, singing, "All five categories, pal.
I find them like bright, flowing gardens, vast
as oceans, deep in each creative feat."
His feet pause. He's listening to something.
I hear it. "Lives progress, become complete
through faith and actions we repeat," I sing
out of the blue. He shoots a laughing glance.
Like O'Connor and Kelly, off we dance.

FOXGLOVE

At distance, they seem a field of beehives
huddled in groups of lily white, soft pink
of roses. Now near: "You kept me alive,
your family here," I whisper. Then sink
hands softly into a chosen cluster,
caress their silk-like flutes. Move my face close
to observe their mouths, tongues holding luster
of dusk, each interior stained with flows
dark red, like blood droplets. I kneel to tell:
"You see, my heart had stopped. The hospital's
emergency room revived the limp shell
of me with digitalis. So I called
the drug firm days later to learn who grew
the crop, then came in love to thank you."

Carolina

at New York's Pane e Cioccolato

The busboy says he's from Puerto Rico,
a town called Carolina, near the coast
just east of San Juan. I say did you know
I'm from Carolina too. It's where ghosts
from the Civil War still haunt Southerners.
"Mine's called La Tierra de Gigantes,"
he says. Smiles slyly. Adds how he prefers
the name his grandmother learned in old days:
El Pueblo de los Tumbabrazos.
He leans down, whispers, "Those who cut arms off."
He moves to a deserted table close
by, grows silent, folding the dry, white cloth.
He wipes the marble tabletop, his hand
cloth-covered: a gull soaring over land

some twenty-thousand feet below. His eyes
explore terrain with a sad stare, making
me feel he's lost, not in legends or lies
he's told me, but in that sudden aching
for home we all have when strangers tap it
loose from deep in our hearts' caverns, like some
phosphorous glow: how stalactites trap it
and hold it below until our eyes come
down to behold it. Perhaps he sees smoke
from his town's factories there in the stone's
brown swirls; or the Loiza River's flow;
or eyes of a lover who's never gone,
though he left her in Carolina years
ago, standing on the runway in tears.

Razglednicas*

for Miklós Radnóti

Fall 1944: I, an infant
crawling on the warm floor in Little Rock,
know nothing of you—shot dead near Abda,
six hundred strides from the Raba. Hemlocks,
huddled bareboned, hide the clumsy mass grave
your fellow Hungarians will find two
years later. In the pocket of your slave-
camp jacket, a palm-sized notebook soaked through
with blood, urine and fertile loam. Poems
somehow survive, taut script of visual
postcards describing your final days: Grim,
dark-rubied visions of your wife, fearful
peasants smoking pipes, captives pissing blood,
Lorsi shot dead, and you soon, in the woods.

Picture postcards in Serbo-Croatian

Subway Strike

My old girlfriend would never ride subways,
terrified it would crack thick scars, release
visions of her mother running away
just as the car door wrenched shut, a wild, pleased
flare to her eyes, glaring back at her child,
five years old and screaming, face and hands pressed
like fresh batter against the window, wild
herself with panic, fear-serrated chest
heaving to spews of vomit as the car
lurched away. The bitch would always relent,
grab a cab to two stops uptown, just far
enough to meet the train, weep and repent
as she'd lift my future love in her arms,
rasp lies of how she really meant no harm.

The Holiest Light

Galileo, his telescope the new
extended eye mapping orbits of stars,
must have whispered to himself, "Dear sir, you
now, both scientist and poet, rise far
too close to heaven. What do you think popes
will say to this sacrilege? Rewrite Church
law for your sake? This curved glass is a rope
they'll use to noose your neck. But let my search
kill both me and their terrifying faith,
strangle their shouts with truth of heaven's face.
Let this universe, as one, form the lathe
which tools all fear into a sacred space
where we speak from hearts: the holiest light."
Our eyes traject our deepest love tonight.

Logic

What is my nature? What is my value?
If my quarks and leptons formed from ocean
and earth—an exploding star's residue,
particles of universal motion—
if my matter's mass mirrors all else in
the cosmos, am I not only part of
the heavens but heaven itself? Essence
of life everywhere? If I fall in love
on clear nights when stars chorus eyes and song
flowing through me, my body imploding
and exploding at once, is that not strong
and weak uniting, gravity's prodding,
electromagnetic charging? Each force
fundamental to each particle's course?

INDEX OF POEM TITLES